WOULD YOU RATHER...

For Kids and Their Adults!

365 Clean and Hilarious Questions the Entire Family Will Love!

CIEL PUBLISHING

INSTRUCTIONS

1. Find some players to play with.

Though we just need two players to get started, the more the merrier!

If you have more than two people, then you can split into teams of two- Team A and Team B.

2. Agree on which team should start.

You can get creative with this (rock-paper-scissors, anyone?)

3. The team that starts has to ask the other team a *Would You Rather* question.

Choose from the many this book provides!

4. The other team must then choose the best option between the two and state why they would choose it.

Trust me, this is usually harder than it seems.

5. Play continues until one of the teams is not able to answer or state why they chose an option.

Or until food is ready. Whichever comes first!

Ready? Get your game face on!

Would You Rather...

1

...give up watching TV / movies for a year or give up playing games for a year?

2

...never be able to eat meat or never be able to eat vegetables?

3

...see what was behind every closed door or be able to guess the combination of every safe on the first try?

4

... have an unlimited international first class ticket or never have to pay for food at restaurants?

Would You Rather…

5

… super sensitive taste or
super sensitive hearing?

6

… get one free round trip international
plane ticket every year or be able to fly
domestic anytime for free?

7

… be balding but fit or overweight with a
full head of hair?

8

…be able to see things that are very far
away, like binoculars or be able to see
things very close up, like a microscope?

Would You Rather…

9

…never be able to drink sodas
like coke again or only be able
to drink sodas and nothing else?

10

…be a practicing doctor or
a medical researcher?

11

…always be able to see 5 minutes into
the future or always be able to see 100
years into the future?

12

…have amazingly fast typing / texting
speed or be able to read ridiculously
fast?

Would You Rather...

13

...be a wizard or a superhero?

14

... fight 100 duck sized horses or 1 horse sized duck?

15

...be a tree or have to live in a tree for the rest of your life?

16

...be a reverse centaur or a reverse mermaid/merman?

Would You Rather…

17

…know the history of every object you touched or be able to talk to animals?

18

… have to announce to everyone around you whenever you have to fart
or pee your pants daily?

19

…have constantly dry eyes
or a constant runny nose?

20

…be a famous director or a famous actor?

Would You Rather...

21

...not be able to open any closed doors (locked or unlocked) or not be able to close any open doors?

22

...give up all drinks except for water or give up eating anything that was cooked in an oven?

23

...have to read aloud every word you read or sing everything you say out loud?

24

...have a completely automated home or a self-driving car?

Would You Rather…

25

…work very hard at a rewarding job
or hardly have to work at a job
that isn't rewarding?

26

…be reincarnated as a fly
or just cease to exist after you die?

27

…be held in high regard by your parents
or your friends?

28

…have one real get out of jail free card
or a key that opens any door?

Would You Rather...

29

...be able to go to any theme park in the world for free for the rest of your life or eat for free at any drive through restaurant for the rest of your life?

30

...be an amazing painter or a brilliant mathematician?

31

...lose the ability to read or lose the ability to speak?

32

...own a mouse or a rat?

Would You Rather...

33

...live in a cave or a tree house?

34

··· go to the moon or go to Mars?

35

...live under a sky with no stars at night
or live under a sky with no clouds
during the day?

36

...never get angry
or never be envious?

Would You Rather…

37

…use a push lawn mower with a bar that is far too high or far too low?

38

…have a piggy bank that doubles any money you put in it or find ten dollars under your pillow every time you wake up?

39

…have free Wi-Fi wherever you go or be able to drink unlimited free coffee at any coffee shop?

40

…live on the beach or in a cabin in the woods?

Would You Rather...

41

...lose your left hand or right foot?

42

...spend the whole day in a huge garden or spend the whole day in a large museum?

43

...be forced to dance every time you hear music or be forced to sing along to every song you hear?

44

...eat a box of dry spaghetti noodles or a cup of uncooked rice?

Would You Rather…

45

…face your fears
or forget that you have them?

46

…abducted by robotic aliens or organic aliens?

47

…be lost in a bad part of town
or lost in the forest?

48

…be born again in a totally different life
or be born again with all the knowledge
you have now?

Would You Rather...

49

...never get a paper cut again or never get something stuck in your eye again?

50

...never lose your phone again or never lose your keys again?

51

...have a flying carpet or a car that can drive underwater?

52

...find five dollars on the ground or find all of your missing socks?

Would You Rather...

53

...be famous but ridiculed
or be just a normal person?

54

...never have another embarrassing fall
in public or never feel the need to pass
gas in public again?

55

...be able to talk to land animals, animals that
fly, or animals that live under the water?

56

...lose your best friend or all of your friends
except for your best friend?

Would You Rather...

57

...never be stuck in traffic again
or never get another cold?

58

...blink at twice the normal rate or not be able
to blink for 5 minutes but then have to close
your eyes for 10 seconds every 5 minutes?

59

··· endless snow or endless rain?

60

...have a bottomless box of Legos
or a bottomless gas tank?

Would You Rather…

61

...every shirt you ever wear to be kind of itchy
or only be able to use extra thin toilet paper?

62

...use eye drops made of vinegar or toilet
paper made from sandpaper?

63

...not be able to see any colors or have mild
but constant tinnitus (ringing in the ears)?

64

...go bald or be forever cursed
to have terrible haircuts?

Would You Rather...

65

...never be able to leave your own country or never be able to fly in an airplane?

66

...have edible spaghetti hair that regrows every night or sweat maple syrup?

67

...have one nipple or two belly buttons?

68

...have no fingers or no elbows?

Would You Rather...

69

...have no fingers or no elbows?

70

...never have a toilet clog on you again
or never have the power go out again?

71

...have all traffic lights you approach be
green or never have to stand in line again?

72

...be in debt for $100,000 or never be able
to make more than $3,500 a month?

Would You Rather…

73

…be the best in the world at climbing trees or the best in the world at jumping rope?

74

…live in a giant desert or a giant dessert?

75

…wake up in the middle of an unknown desert or wake up in a row boat on an unknown body of water?

76

…have everything you draw become real but be terrible at drawing or be able to fly but only as fast as you can walk?

Would You Rather…

77

…only be able to walk on all fours or only be able to walk sideways like a crab?

78

…never run out of battery power for whatever phone and tablet you own or always have free Wi-Fi wherever you go?

79

…live a comfortable and peaceful life in the woods in a small cabin or a life full of conflict in a mansion in a city?

80

…have all of your clothes fit perfectly or have the most comfortable pillow, blankets, and sheets in existence?

Would You Rather...

81

...never sweat again or never feel cold again?

82

...be covered in fur or covered in scales?

83

...be able to create a new holiday
or create a new sport?

84

...eat an egg with a half formed chicken inside
or eat five cooked cockroaches?

Would You Rather...

85

...wear a wedding dress / tuxedo every single day or wear a bathing suit every single day?

86

...be an unimportant character in the last movie you saw or an unimportant character in the last book you read?

87

...move to a new city or town every week or never be able to leave the city or town you were born in?

88

...live in a house shaped like a circle or a house shaped like a triangle?

Would You Rather…

89

...live in a place with a lot of trees
or live in a place near the ocean?

90

...do school work as a group or by yourself?

91

...your only mode of transportation
be a donkey or a giraffe?

92

...be able to do flips and backflips
or break dance?

Would You Rather...

93
...eat spoonful of wasabi
or a spoonful of Tabasco sauce?

94
...eat a ketchup sandwich
or a Siracha sandwich?

95
...only be able to drink from a straw
or only be able to use a spoon (no fork)?

96
...travel for 5 years in an RV
or travel for 5 years in a sailboat?

Would You Rather...

97

...inherit 20 million dollars or earn 50 million dollars through your hard work?

98

...do a TED talk or sing a song on stage at a concert with your favorite singer?

99

... travel the world for a year on a shoe string budget or stay in only one country for a year but live in luxury?

100

...have a magic carpet that flies or a see-through submarine?

Would You Rather...

101

...live without hot water for showers / baths or live without a washing machine?

102

...always feel like someone is following you but no one is or have someone always follow you but never notice?

103

...have a horribly corrupt government or no government?

104

...live the next 10 years of your life in China or Russia?

Would You Rather...

105

...travel the world for a year all expenses paid or have $50,000 to spend on whatever you want?

106

...be unable to move your body every time it rains or not be able to stop moving while the sun is out?

107

...have no eyebrows or only one eyebrow?

108

...only wear one color each day or have to wear seven colors each day?

Would You Rather…

109

... have all dogs try to attack you when they see you or all birds try to attack you when they see you?

110

...be unable to have kids or only be able to conceive quintuplets?

111

...eat rice with every meal or eat bread with every meal?

112

...never be able to wear pants or never be able to wear shorts?

Would You Rather...

113

...know all the mysteries of the universe or know the outcome of every choice you make?

114

...have out of control body hair
or out of control body odor?

115

...have chapped lips that never heal or a terrible dandruff that can't be treated?

116

...be able to jump as far as a kangaroo or hold your breath as long as a whale?

Would You Rather…

117

…spend the rest of your life with a sailboat as your home or an RV as your home?

118

… be completely insane and know that you are insane or be completely insane and believe you are sane?

119

…be an average person in the present or a king 2500 years ago?

120

…have the police hunting you for a murder you didn't commit or a psychopathic clown hunting you?

Would You Rather…

121

...be a bowling champion
or a curling champion?

122

...be so afraid of heights that you can't go
to the second floor of a building or be so
afraid of the sun that you can only leave
the house on rainy days?

123

... have 20 butterflies instantly appear
from nowhere every time you cough or
have 100 butterflies die somewhere in
the world every time you cough?

124

... always wear earmuffs or a nose plug?

Would You Rather…

125

…be fantastic at riding horses
or amazing at driving dirt bikes?

equestrian

126

…become twice as strong when you stick
your fingers on both of your ears or crawl
twice as fast as you can run?

127

…know the uncomfortable truth of the
world or believe a comforting lie?

128

…be fluent in 10 languages or be able to code
in 10 different programming languages?

Would You Rather...

129

...be incredibly funny or incredibly smart?

130

... Have all conspiracy theories be true or live in a world where no leaders really know what they are doing?

131

...have every cat or dog that gets lost end up at your house or have your friends' dirty laundry teleported to your house?

132

...have earbuds and headphones never sit right on / in your ears or have all music either slightly too quiet or slightly too loud?

Would You Rather...

133

...get 5 dollars for every song you sing in public
or 50 dollars for every stranger you kiss?

134

...brush your teeth with soap
or drink sour milk?

135

...snitch on your best friend for a crime
they committed or go to jail for
the crime they committed?

136

...be married to a 10 with a bad personality
or a 6 with an amazing personality?

Would You Rather...

137

...have skin that changes color based on your emotions or have tattoos appear all over your body depicting what you did yesterday?

138

···have the power to gently nudge anyone's decisions or have complete puppet master control of five people?

139

...fart every time you have a serious conversation or burp after every kiss?

140

...live in a utopia as a normal person or in a dystopia as the supreme ruler?

Would You Rather…

141

...be able to be free from ads on social media or be free from email spam for the rest of your life?

142

...be beautiful / handsome but stupid or intelligent but ugly?

143

... lose all of your memories from birth to now or lose your ability to make new long term memories?

144

...be infamous in history books or be forgotten after your death?

Would You Rather...

145

...never have to work again or never have to sleep again (you won't feel tired or suffer negative health effects)?

146

... be able to control animals (but not humans) with your mind or control electronics with your mind?

147

... suddenly be elected a senator or suddenly become a CEO of a major company?

148

...donate your body to science or donate your organs to people who need them?

Would You Rather...

149

...go back to age 5 with everything you know now or know now everything your future self will learn?

150

... sell all of your possessions or sell one of your organs?

151

...relive the same day for 365 days or lose a year of your life?

152

...have a golden voice or a silver tongue?

Would You Rather…

153

… be unable to use search engines
or unable to use social media?

154

… give up bathing for a month
or give up the internet for a month?

155

…have unlimited sushi for life
or unlimited tacos for life?

156

… have hands that kept growing as you got
older or feet that kept growing
as you got older?

Would You Rather...

157

... have everything you eat be too salty or not salty enough no matter how much salt you add?

158

... never be able to use a touchscreen or never be able to use a keyboard and mouse?

159

... be transported permanently 500 years into the future or 500 years into the past?

160

... be able to control fire or water?

Would You Rather…

161

…know when you are going to die
or how you are going to die?

162

…be feared by all or loved by all?

163

… be able to teleport anywhere
or be able to read minds?

164

… find your true love or a suitcase
with five million dollars inside?

Would You Rather…

165

… live without the internet
or live without AC and heating?

166

… be poor but help people
or become incredibly rich by hurting people?

167

… be locked in a room that is constantly
dark for a week or a room that is
constantly bright for a week?

168

… have a horrible short term memory or a
horrible long term memory?

Would You Rather…

169

… be completely invisible for one day or be able to fly for one day?

170

… be the first person to explore a planet or be the inventor of a drug that cures a deadly disease?

171

… have an easy job working for someone else or work for yourself but work incredibly hard?

172

… never use social media sites / apps again or never watch another movie or TV show?

Would You Rather...

173

... be alone for the rest of your life or always be surrounded by annoying people?

174

... live your entire life in a virtual reality where all your wishes are granted or in the real world?

175

... die in 20 years with no regrets or die in 50 years with many regrets?

176

... your shirts be always two sizes too big or one size too small?

Would You Rather...

177

... famous when you are alive and forgotten when you die or unknown when you are alive but famous after you die?

178

... be able to see 10 minutes into your own future or 10 minutes into the future of anyone but yourself?

179

... lose all of your money and valuables or all of the pictures you have ever taken?

180

... always be 10 minutes late or always be 20 minutes early?

Would You Rather...

181

... live in the wilderness far from civilization
or live on the streets of a city as
a homeless person?

182

...watch the big game at home
or live at the stadium?

183

...be too busy or be too bored?

184

... be your own boss
or work for someone else?

Would You Rather...

185

... hear the good news
or the bad news first?

186

... have nosy neighbors
or noisy neighbors?

187

... be proposed to in private
or in front of family and friends?

188

... have to sew all your clothes
or grow your own food?

Would You Rather...

189

... live at the top of a tall NYC apartment building or at the top of a mountain?

190

... have Rambo or The Terminator on your side?

191

... be on a survival reality show or dating game show?

192

... be an Olympic gold medalist or a Nobel Peace Prize winner?

Would You Rather...

193
... be a master at origami
or a master of sleight of hand magic?

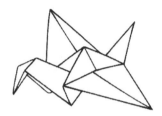

194

... have a desk job
or an outdoor job?

195

... have a 10-hour dinner with a headstrong
politician from an opposing party, or attend a
10-hour concert for a music group you detest?

196

... be the youngest or the oldest sibling?`

Would You Rather...

197

... have a cook or a maid?

198

... eat a whole raw onion
or a whole lemon?

199

... be stuck on an island alone
or with someone who talks incessantly?

200

... get rich through hard work or through
winning the lottery?

Would You Rather...

201

...work in a group or work alone?

202

... eat a meal of cow tongue
or octopus?

203

... have x-ray vision
or magnified hearing?

204

...never have any homework or be paid
10$ per hour for doing your homework?

Would You Rather...

205

... be a kid your whole life
or an adult your whole life?

206

... go deep sea diving or bungee jumping?

207

... explore space or the ocean?

208

... spend the night in a luxury hotel room
or camping surrounded by beautiful scenery?

Would You Rather...

209

... put a stop to war
or end world hunger?

210

... be the most popular person at work
or school or be the smartest?

211

... go on a cruise with friends
or with your spouse?

212

...read an awesome book
or watch a good movie?

Would You Rather…

213

…make a phone call or send a text?

214

… go to the movies alone
or to dinner alone?

215

…receive cash
or gifts for your birthday?

216

… be stuck on a broken ski lift
or in a broken elevator?

Would You Rather...

217

... listen to music from the 70's
or music from today?

218

...be Batman or Spiderman?

219

... become someone else
or just stay you?

220

... always say everything on your mind
or never speak again?

Would You Rather...

221

... lose your vision or your hearing?

222

... work more hours per day, but fewer
days or work fewer hours per day,
but more days?

223

... be without internet for a week,
or without your phone for a week?

224

... feel worse if no one showed up to your
wedding or to your funeral?

Would You Rather...

225

... win the lottery or live twice as long?

226

... be able to talk with animals
or speak all foreign languages?

227

... have a rewind button
or a pause button on your life?

228

... have more time or more money?

Would You Rather…

229

… go into the past and meet your ancestors or go into the future and meet your great-great grandchildren?

230

… be outside all day
or inside all day?

231

… go to the dentist
or go to the doctor?

232

… have a pet cat
or a pet dog?

Would You Rather…

233

… jump into a pool of chocolate pudding
or a pool of chocolate ice cream?

234

… help set the table before dinner
or help clean up after dinner?

235

…stay up late or get up early?

236

… be really tall or really short?

Would You Rather...

237

... be super strong or superfast?

238

...only be able to whisper
or only be able to shout?

239

... stay at your current age
or be 10 years older?

240

... be the most popular kid in school
or the smartest kid in school?

Would You Rather…

241

… get good grades or be a good athlete?

242

… have a personal life-sized robot
or a jetpack?

243

… meet George Washington,
or the current President?

244

… be a chef or a waiter/waitress?

Would You Rather...

245

... be a teacher or a janitor?

246

...be a firefighter or a police officer?

247

...only be able to eat your favorite food for
the rest of your life or never eat
your favorite food again?

248

...be a doctor or a garbage man?

Would You Rather...

249

...have fries
or cookies?

250

...eat pizza
or hot dogs?

251

...eat chips
or candy?

252

...live in an amusement park
or a zoo?

Would You Rather...

253

... sneeze cheese
or have your tears be chocolate flavored?

254

... have 500 spiders in your bedroom
or 1000 grasshoppers in the rest of the house?

255

...have five stitches to fix a bad cut
or have a tooth pulled?

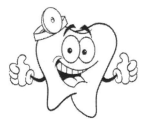

256

... be a straight A student with no social
life or be the most popular kid in school
with poor grades?

Would You Rather...

257

... jump into a pool of chocolate pudding
or a pool of mud?

258

...lick the bottom of your shoe
or eat your boogers?

259

...eat tacos or pizza?

260

...eat a dead bug or a live worm?

Would You Rather...

261

...have cookies or cake?

262

...have an unlimited amount of chips
or soda?

263

...play video games or play outside?

264

... suffer from spontaneous shouting
or unpredictable fainting spells?

Would You Rather...

265

...wear clown makeup every day for a year
or wear a tutu every day for a year?

266

...not be allowed to wash your hands for a
month or your hair for a month?

267

... drink all your food from a baby bottle
or wear visible diapers for the rest of your life?

268

... always speak in rhymes
or sing instead of speak?

Would You Rather...

269

... sit with a resting lion for ten minutes
or run across a hungry alligator's back?

270

... surf in shark-infested waters
or jump free fall with a parachute into the
Grand Canyon?

271

... have a pig nose or a monkey face?

272

... always smell rotting meat
or always smell skunk?

Would You Rather…

273

… have your grandmother's hairstyle
or first name?

274

… have a horse's tail
or a unicorn horn?

275

… have hands instead of feet
or feet instead of hands?

276

… always have to skip everywhere
or run everywhere?

Would You Rather...

277

... eat a bowl of spaghetti noodles without sauce or a bowl of spaghetti sauce without noodles?

278

... hold a snake or kiss a jellyfish?

279

... watch a two-hour movie or watch two hours of shows?

280

... eat a bowl of spaghetti that was just one long noodle or eat ice cream launched from a catapult?

Would You Rather...

281

... have fireworks go off every evening for an hour or have Christmas three times a year?

282

... have an elephant-sized cat or a cat-sized elephant?

283

...be a falcon or a dolphin?

284

... eat a small can of cat food or eat two rotten tomatoes?

Would You Rather…

285

… go to the doctor for a shot
or the dentist to get a cavity filled?

286

… go camping
or stay in a hotel room?

287

…drink orange juice or milk?

288

… be the fastest swimmer on earth
or the fastest runner on earth?

Would You Rather...

289

...read a book or read a magazine?

290

... get a new pair of shoes or a jacket?

291

... go to the beach or go to the zoo?

292

... be given every Lego set that was ever made
or get every new Lego set that
comes out for free?

Would You Rather...

293

... have everything you draw become real or become a superhero of your choice?

294

... have a real triceratops or a robot triceratops? (Both are the same size.)

295

... be able to make plants grow very quickly or be able to make it rain whenever you wanted?

296

... play in a giant mud puddle or a pool?

Would You Rather...

297

... be a famous musician
or a famous business owner?

298

... have an amazing tree house
or your whole yard be a trampoline?

299

... have a pet dinosaur of your choice
or a dragon the size of a dog?

300

... have 100$ now
or 1000$ in a year?

Would You Rather...

301

... be able to talk to animals
or be able to fly?

302

... eat your favorite food every day or find 5
dollars under your pillow every morning?

303

... learn to surf
or learn to ride a skateboard?

304

...have a pet penguin
or a pet Komodo dragon?

Would You Rather…

305

…hang out for an hour with 10 puppies
or 10 kittens?

306

… have a very powerful telescope
or a very powerful microscope?

307

… be a scientist
or be the boss of a company?

308

… be the fastest kid at your school
or the smartest kid at your school?

Would You Rather...

309

... be able to change colors like a chameleon or hold your breath underwater for an hour?

310

... eat broccoli flavored ice cream or meat flavored cookies?

311

... have the power to shrink things to half their size or the power to enlarge things to twice their size?

312

... play on swings or play on a slide?

Would You Rather...

313

... not need to eat and never be hungry or not need to drink and never be thirsty?

314

... get to name a newly discovered tree or a newly discovered spider?

315

... have no homework or no tests?

316

... swim in Jell-O or swim in Nutella?

Would You Rather...

317

...never be able to eat any type meat again
or never be able to eat things
with sugar in them?

318

... have a 3d printer
or the best phone on the market?

319

... dance or draw?

320

... drive a race car
or fly a helicopter?

Would You Rather…

321

… be unable to control how fast you talk
or unable to control how loud you talk?

322

… live in a house in the forest where
there aren't many people around or live in
a city with lots of people around?

323

… be rich and unknown or be famous and
have enough money, but not be rich?

324

… have pancakes every day for breakfast
or pizza every day for dinner?

Would You Rather...

325

... go snow skiing
or water skiing?

326

... move to a country and city of your
choice or stay in your own country but
not be able to decide where you moved?

327

... be able to learn everything in a book by
putting it under your pillow while you slept or
be able to control your dreams every night?

328

... have a jetpack or a hoverboard that
actually hovers (no wheels)?

Would You Rather...

329

... never have to take a bath/shower but still always smell nice or never have to get another shot but still be healthy?

330

... be able to eat any spicy food without a problem or never be bitten by another mosquito?

331

... have a ten dollar bill or ten dollars in coins?

332

... ride a camel or ride a horse?

Would You Rather...

333

... ride in a hang glider or skydive?

334

...play soccer or baseball?

335

...live in a castle
or a spaceship traveling far from earth?

336

... be really good at skateboarding
or really good at any video game you tried?

Would You Rather…

337

… have a room with whiteboard walls that you can draw on or a room where the whole ceiling is one big skylight?

338

… lay in a bathtub filled with worms for 5 minutes or lay in a bathtub filled with beetles that don't bite for 5 minutes?

339

… have a house with trampoline floors or a house with aquarium floors?

340

… be able to see new colors that no other people could see or be able to hear things that no other humans can hear?

Would You Rather...

341

... be a cyborg or a robot?

342

... have a private movie theater
or your own private arcade?

343

... be able to type faster than anyone
or speak faster than anyone?

344

... control the outcome of any coin flip
or be unbeatable at rock, paper, scissors?

Would You Rather...

345

... eat a turkey sandwich with vanilla ice cream inside or eat vanilla ice cream with bits of turkey inside?

346

... visit every country in the World or be able to play any musical instrument?

347

... ride a roller coaster or go down a giant water slide?

348

... go on vacation to a new country every summer vacation or get an extra three weeks of summer break?

Would You Rather...

349

... have a jetpack
or a jet?

350

...be able to talk to dogs
or cats?

351

...be an actor/actress in a movie or write a
movie script that would be made into a movie?

352

... have 10 mosquito bites or 1 bee sting?

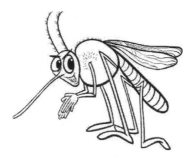

Would You Rather...

353

... an amazing photographer
or an amazing writer?

354

... be able to remember everything in
every book you read or remember every
conversation you have?

355

... sneeze uncontrollably for 15 minutes once
every day or sneeze once every 3 minutes of
the day while you are awake?

356

... eat smores
or cupcakes?

Would You Rather…

357

… move to a different city
or move to a different country?

358

… have super strong arms
or super strong legs??

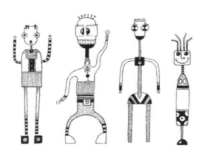

359

… be amazing at drawing and painting or be
able to remember everything you ever read?

360

… ride a roller coaster or see a movie?

Would You Rather…

361

… have an unlimited supply of ice cream
or a popular ice cream flavor named after you?

362

… open one 5$ present every day or one
big present that costs between 100$ to
300$ once a month?

Would You Rather...

363

... be able to change the color of anything with just a thought or know every language that has ever been spoken on Earth?

364

... be able to find anything that was lost or every time you touched someone they would be unable to lie?

365

... never have to sleep or never have to eat?

Congratulations for Making It to the End!

I hope you enjoyed these *365 Would You Rather's*.

You now know more epic scenarios than most human beings in the planet!

How does that feel?

Go ahead and spread your new knowledge with friends and family members.

They will thank you for it!

Best-Selling Titles by the Author:

Rubik's Cube Solution Guide for Kids (3x3x3 and 2x2x2) in Full Color
http://bit.ly/Rubiks4Kids

Riddles for Kids: 365 Riddles for Daily Laughs and Giggles
http://bit.ly/RiddlesKids

First Word Search for Kids: 101 Fun with Sight Words, Early Nouns, Phonics & More!
http://bit.ly/FirstWordSearch

Inspiring Quotes for Kids: A Children's Coloring Book
http://bit.ly/InspiringQ

Dragon Coloring Book: Zen Dragons
http://bit.ly/DragonColor

And lastly... If you liked this book, please leave a review!

Amazon reviews from our readers help us keep producing quality content. We're counting with yours!

Thanks!

Made in the USA
Middletown, DE
29 November 2020